C000121245

SILENT PRAYER

by
Fr Andrzej Muszala

*All booklets are published thanks to the
generous support of the members of the
Catholic Truth Society*

CATHOLIC TRUTH SOCIETY
PUBLISHERS TO THE HOLY SEE

Contents

All rights reserved. First published 2016 by The Incorporated Catholic Truth Society, 40-46 Harleyford Road London SE11 5AY Tel: 020 7640 0042 Fax: 020 7640 0046. © 2016 Fr Andrzej Muszala.

ISBN 978 1 78469 130 1

INTRODUCTION

Now once Jesus was in a certain place praying, and when he had finished, one of his disciples said, "Lord, teach us how to pray...." (Lk 11:1)

The request of Jesus's disciple echoes throughout the centuries. Even in our day and age, many men and women, young and old, turn to all kinds of teachers for instruction or apprenticeship in the art and discipline of prayer. Prayer is not just an activity like any other; it touches me in the depths of my being, in that secret sanctuary where I am simply myself face to face with the living God. To pray is not to fly off to the skies or to other galaxies, embellishing or reinventing ourselves; it is to plumb the deepest caverns of *who* and *where* we are.

Father Andrzej Muszala's little book, *Silent Prayer*, is an excellent guide to the first steps of the journey of prayer. It starts with the chapter, "The beginning of prayer", not because it is concerned only with the beginning of prayer but because prayer is a never-ending beginning, and the "first steps" are what keep us on the right way.

Prayer is a total act of the human person; all the levels and aspects of my being are involved, from the muscles of my body ("Closing your eyes"), to my imagination ("Looking at Jesus"), to my understanding ("Spiritual reading"), all the way to the "act of faith" through which I am in contact with God Himself. It is this act of faith which attains to the very "Presence of God" in ourselves and in creation.

We are reminded that the act of faith is the essential act of prayer. Everything else is a means; everything else is secondary and accidental. The act of faith may be dark but it is also certain and its certitude finds rest and comfort in God's promises. God is *always* touched by the act of faith and this is the fundamental certitude of prayer. This certitude should be translated in an attitude of hope and trust in our everyday life and work. "If God is for us, who can be against us?" (*Rm* 8:31). This certitude is the source of great joy.

Eduardo José Calasanz teaches Philosophy and Letters at the Ateneo de Manila University (Philippines) where he also serves as Associate Dean for Academic Affairs.

PART ONE:
WHAT IS SILENT PRAYER?

Do you want to learn to pray? Then pray!
(St Teresa of Avila)

1. The beginning of prayer

What do we think of when we refer to *interior prayer* or *silent prayer*? We have many ways of describing what we mean by prayer: communication with God, a form of request, adoration or thanksgiving, a conversation with God or even a *monologue*. We may even regard praying as a means of achieving merit! It is astonishing how complicated we can make prayer seem! No wonder we get tired and abandon the attempt!

Perhaps it is time to return to the example of those great Doctors of the Church who made their spiritual journey in the past and had knowledge and experience of prayer: St Teresa of Avila, St John of the Cross and St Thérèse of Lisieux.

St Teresa of Avila was able to describe prayer as nothing other than a close sharing between friends: "being on terms of friendship with God, with Him Who, we know, loves us" (*The Life*, VIII, 7). For her, words, however beautifully crafted, were not necessary. Wasn't it Jesus Himself who said, "In your prayers do not babble as the gentiles do, for they think that by using many words they will make themselves heard." (*Mt* 6:7-8a).

In her view, the essence of prayer is to *love* a lot, not to *talk* a lot, just like two people sitting together, in silence, bonded by their love for each other like a husband and wife: the *beloved* and the *bride*. In order to "be with God" we do not have to say anything! Our presence is enough for Him! FOR HIM!

But we are not accustomed to spending time with God, in silence, without any specific words or intentions. We feel more comfortable *saying* something! We feel we must tell Him about the Church's needs, the world's needs, our own needs! Then we feel we have achieved something; we have taken action; we have shown concern for God's issues. We have not *wasted our time*! Silent prayer obliges us to leave all that to the Almighty!

To enter into silent prayer we must leave everything behind. All must be still and silent so that we can prepare to open our soul for the presence and the action of the Holy Trinity. We have to give God the time to act upon us and transform us into His own image which is what He wishes to do. This is difficult because I am not used to doing this. I do not dare to allow God to act; to act within my soul and to make changes. I will not say it out loud but I know that God is dangerous, that He is unpredictable and that if I allow Him to act, God could do something I may not like!

Perhaps that's why silent prayer is not that popular!

Bearing all this in mind, would you be prepared to spend some time in silence, in the presence of God? If you agree to do so, how long must you stay? Jesus chided the disciples who were not able to stay awake with Him for one hour (*Mt* 26:40). Well, maybe a whole hour is out of the question; give Him half an hour then. Even so it seems an age to spend in total silence. How do you spend such a long time? What can you do?

You can use the Gospels to help you. Read a few sentences slowly and repeatedly. Keep these sentences in your mind and believe that this is Jesus, whispering them in your soul. Try to think only about Him and His presence in the depths of your soul. If you feel you have to say something, just say "I believe". That is enough! Remain like this for the rest of the time.

2. How to pray

What you do and how you behave while you are praying is important, otherwise you run the risk of turning your prayer into a form of selfishness. Prayer is like climbing in order to reach the summit of the "Mount of Love". The path leading to the summit is steep. Once you are on this path you have to forget about yourself and be open to God's will. The ascent needs planning and clear instructions. Our mountain guide is St John of the Cross who gave clear instructions in *The Ascent of Mount Carmel*. If you follow them carefully, you will not get lost!

He describes three paths leading to the summit. The first path is "the path of earthly attainments". Those who take this path are seeking all kinds of personal and material benefits; they are imposing their *own will* on God. This path is called "I am thinking about myself".

The second path is "the path of heavenly attainments and spiritual consolations". Those who take this path are looking for God's revelations, consolations, positive feelings and happiness. They too simply think of themselves.

Neither of these groups of climbers is nearing the summit. They are getting lost amidst their own desires. They are not even half way along the path to the summit and it is so crowded out there!

The third and true way is a path that we can call "The Five Nothings"!

This is the "narrow gate and narrow road that leads to life" (*Mt* 7:14) which only a few souls find. This is the path for you and me to take if we want to reach the summit and unite with God. This is a path for those who are crazy enough to take the risk. This is a path for people seeking God Himself and only His will. This is the path you can take today to meet God. You can meet your Beloved today in your silent prayer.

What are the five "Nothings" that we must seek?

The First Nothing: *Standing in the presence of God*

Think about the fact that Jesus lives in you. In fact, the Holy Trinity is hidden deep in your soul, but to find God there, your soul has to concentrate!

> The Word, the Son of God, together with the Father and the Holy Spirit, is hidden in essence and in presence, in the inmost being of the soul. That soul, therefore, that will find Him, must go out from all things in will and affection, and enter into the profoundest self-recollection. (St John of the Cross, *Spiritual Canticle*, 1:7)

- At the beginning of your prayer forget about your own issues.
- Concentrate only on this most important truth: GOD LIVES IN YOU!
- Leave everything behind, your desires, senses, reason, will and memory.
- Direct them from the external world to God's world.

The Second Nothing: *Spiritual reading*

- It is Jesus, not you, who leads your prayer.
- Therefore open the Bible now and read.
- Read slowly.
- Allow some breaks.
- Read with your heart.
- You are reading His letter to you.
- Open yourself to His presence!

The Third Nothing: *Closing your eyes*

- This is practical advice from St Teresa of Avila.
- This simple gesture is very helpful to stop you looking around at the outside world.
- This gesture helps you to enter God's world.
- With your heart open you can find your Beloved in your soul.

The Fourth Nothing: *Looking at Jesus*

This is looking at Jesus with your heart in a particular scenario that you have read about in the Bible (e.g. when He is in the desert or at Cana in Galilee or talking to Nicodemus at night).

- Look at Him as you would look at a beloved person.
- Look at Him and allow yourself to be with Him.
- To enter into contact with Him.

The Fifth Nothing: *Making your act of faith*

You make your act of faith by:

- giving yourself totally;
- loving without any boundaries;
- being grateful to Him for allowing you to be with Him;
- trusting Him entirely and putting yourself into His hands.

There you reach the summit of the Mount we were talking about. You are united with Jesus - your beloved One and with the Holy Trinity. Rest in that state as long as you can!

With these simple steps you can follow Jesus and His path. This is not a new technique but it helps you to forget about yourself and to allow Him to act in you. It is Jesus who is praying to His Father inside your soul. It is He who is acting and transforming you.

3. God's presence

God is *here!* God lives in everyone. He even lives in the person who does not believe in Him. This is where silent prayer truly starts. God is *within*, in each of us, in the depths of our souls. This is where we should seek Him, not somewhere else.

> He penetrates us and envelops us. There is not a molecule of our being where He is not; there is no movement of our members nor of our faculties that He has not animated. He is around us and even in those regions more intimate and more profound than our soul itself. God is the soul of our soul, the life of our life. (P. Marie-Eugen OCD, *I Want to See God,* I,2,A,I)

Let us try to touch God today by our prayer, our faith and our love. Let us take a journey inside our souls where He has always been living and discover the first "nothing".

When you close your eyes and concentrate, you will find His secret presence. God is there, inside you, full of His life. It is very hard to feel Him because He is in the very centre of your soul where neither your physical nor mystical senses can reach. But nevertheless that is the truth!

In order to describe the Kingdom of God, Jesus spoke in parables and used simple descriptions and comparisons to help us to understand. Let us follow His example to understand what is happening incessantly inside each of us.

GOD IS THE TRINITY. This means LIFE: that is: birth-death-and-resurrection.

God is LOVE. His love is inside us *pulsing* all the time.

The heart is the most important organ in the human body and it beats constantly from the second month after conception until death; a seventy-year-old heart has beaten more than two billion times. Every second, blood is pumped out and spreads to all the organs in the body to give the oxygen and nutrients which are needed to stay alive. The heart is beating all the time. The heart never stops working. What kind of machinery could do the same job? Touch your pulse and think about this invisible, anonymous "friend" to whom you are indebted for your life. Have you ever seen your heart? It is the most humble and well-hidden organ in the body, but it performs an immense task. Close your eyes and "look" at your heart.

The heart is the image of God the Father. Although you do not realise it, He is inside your soul. He is the invisible and humble Father, "pulsing" within you every moment, pouring out His Son, "a thousand times a second", in fact *beyond* time, that is to say *eternally*. The Son is being generated all the time. The Father is whispering, "You are my Son, today I have begotten you." In begetting Him, the Father is giving us His Son. He is not keeping anything for Himself but He is passing to His Son all His nature, divinity, essence and life. "All mine is thine, and thine is mine" (Jn 17,10). The Father never stops begetting His Son… Nothing can stop Him doing this.

Blood is transmitted to the whole body, to every single part, even to the most remote organs. It does not miss any cell but reaches each one in order to "die" there - I mean to give everything to the cell - oxygen and nutrients. The blood gives itself completely, without keeping anything to itself, because it "knows" that this is the job assigned to it in order for the cell to live ("I have come so that the sheep may have life and have it to the full" - Jn 10:10). Then the blood comes back to the heart.

The blood is the image of the Son. Just as blood is pumped out from the heart, so God's Son is sent by the Father to every soul to repeat there what happened on Good Friday; the giving of His life for each one of us. While dying He says, "This is my blood shed for you" and thanks to His death, souls can live. In the same way as the blood returns to the heart, the Son comes back to His Father. And what does the Father do? He sends the Son out to the Holy Spirit in order that the Spirit may give new life to the Son. Just as the blood is "revived" in the lungs by getting new oxygen, so Jesus is now handed over to the Holy Spirit who breathes new life into the Son and *resurrects* Him. The lungs are the image of the Holy Spirit (*Pneuma*), who once swept over the waters and now, like a breeze, awakes the Son from the sleep of death. The resurrected Son then comes back to the Father, not to stay with Him, but to be *pumped out* again and to give Himself and everything He owns to the cells, again and again.

This happens constantly.

In you, Jesus LIVES, DIES AND IS RAISED FROM THE DEAD incessantly. It happens whenever you sleep, work, relax or pray. It happens whether you know it or not. He performs, in you, His never-ending act of PASSOVER, through death into real life. The Holy Trinity is inside you, ceaselessly "pulsing" its inner life.

This is just an image but an image of the most profound reality which is constantly being performed inside your soul. Even now at the very moment you are reading these words! This is the God you touch through your interior prayer. You meet a LIVING God. You meet God who IS in the centre of your soul. Prayer, especially interior prayer, acts as a link between you and God. This is the prayer which enables you to seek God and strive towards meeting Him, touching Him with faith and love in order to possess Him and to be submerged in Him. "The property of love is to desire to be united, joined and made equal and like to the object of its love." (St John of the Cross, *Dark Night of the Soul*, 2:13,9)

I would like you to concentrate on this truth when you pray.

Try to concentrate on this truth.

Sometimes only say: "I believe!"

Do it every day - for half an hour as we agreed.

I will be there with you.

We will be there in God together.

4. Spiritual reading

"It is from the Gospels that I find most help in the time of prayer; from them I draw all that I need for my poor soul. I am always discovering in them new lights and hidden mysterious meanings." (St Thérèse of Lisieux, *Manuscript A*, 83vº)

These are the words of another guide to the Mount of Love - St Thérèse of the Child Jesus. This young girl, who had no regular access to spiritual texts, made her own version of the four Gospels in small notebooks which she carried constantly next to her heart, reading them frequently and using them to pray.

At the very end of her "Manuscripts" she wrote:

As Our Lord is now in Heaven, I can only follow Him by the footprints He has left - footprints full of life, full of fragrance. I have only to open the Holy Gospels and at once I breathe the perfume of Jesus, and then I know which way to run; and it is not to the first place, but to the last, that I hasten. I leave the Pharisee to go up, and full of confidence I repeat the humble prayer of the Publican. Above all I follow Magdalen, for the amazing, rather I should say, the loving audacity, that delights the Heart of Jesus, has cast its spell upon mine. (St Thérèse of Lisieux, *Manuscript C*, 37r°)

To be open to the word is essential in silent prayer. This is the second "nothing". It shows you the path. So, when you start your prayer and you are standing in the presence of God, open your Gospel.

Read it slowly, dwelling on each point.

Do not read too much.

Receive the text just like the Old Testament's prophet who was told to *swallow the Scripture piece by piece.* You are now in God's world. By this reading you are becoming familiar with His character. You are getting to know His thinking, reactions and values and you are absorbing and connecting with Him.

When you read, try not to bother about learning something new, or finding some lights from God. Try not to interpret God's will towards you. If you do that you will be concentrating on *yourself.* God will tell you what is needed when He wants to do so. Let Him act. All you need to do is to read.

Jesus said: "Anyone who loves me, will keep my word, and my Father will love him, and we shall come to him and make a home in him" (*Jn* 14:23).

Spiritual reading is the condition necessary for the presence of the Trinity to become real and transforming in you and me. BECAUSE JESUS IS GOD'S WORD!

This Word became flesh. All who have received it have been given the gift of becoming the children of God. It means that whenever you read the Gospel, you not only become acquainted with God, but *you and He are one!* It is like receiving a letter from the one you love. You read the letter so many times that you know the contents of the letter by heart. And even after that, you read the letter again, not to learn something new, but to *absorb the one you love.* Your loved one is living in the words and sentences which are written. Only the insider can read between the lines the most important message, written in invisible ink: "I love you. I miss you".

This is precisely what St Thérèse was writing about - the hidden and mystical meaning of God's Word. Following these footprints, you will quickly begin to ascend the steep path in order to come to union with God at the summit. So, look for Jesus on every page of the Gospel. Let your Gospel reading during your prayer have only one aim: to help you to make contact with Him in order to meet Him personally. And help you love the Beloved.

Simple souls cannot understand complicated methods, and, as I am one of their number, Our Lord has inspired me with a very simple way of fulfilling my obligations. One day, after Holy Communion, He made me understand these words of the Canticles: "Draw me: we will run after Thee to the odour of Thy ointments" (*Sg* 1:4). O my Jesus, there is no need to say: "In drawing me, draw also the souls that I love": these words, "Draw me," suffice. When a soul has let herself be taken captive by the inebriating odour of Thy perfumes, she cannot run alone; as a natural consequence of her attraction towards Thee, the souls of all those she loves are drawn in her train. (St Thérèse of Lisieux, *Manuscript C*, 33v°-34r°)

Let yourself be drawn by the Beloved today. And if you say that you still cannot pray in silence, read His *Word* slowly…

This is all you need.

5. Closing your eyes

The longer you pray the longer you remain in your interior self. Therefore in the third "nothing" you close the gates of your external senses in order to concentrate on God who is living inside your soul. St Teresa of Avila commented that in silent prayer the eyes close themselves. It happens spontaneously in order to restrict all distractions which suddenly appear whenever you start your prayer and are just like flies buzzing around your head. They attack you with double strength, trying to pull you back to the outside world.

Sometimes they are strong enough to discourage you from continuing your prayer. How do you deal with distractions? First of all, close the gates of the outside senses: eyes, ears, taste, touch and smell. Turn off the sources: the noise, voices, music and pictures. Enter the darkness and silence. Do not be afraid. Do not run away! Stay, even if you do not feel comfortable there. The world of the spirit is not familiar to you yet, but if, at the start, you are not discouraged, you will slowly adjust to it.

It will take time for you to become familiar with that world but that is because you have never before tried to feel at home in the depths of your soul.

One difficulty alone remains: though He is within, yet He is hidden. So you, if you will find Him, must forget all that is yours, withdraw from all created things, and hide yourself in the secret retreat of the spirit, shutting the door upon yourself - that is, denying your will in all things - and praying to your Father in secret. Then you, being hidden with Him, will be conscious of His presence in secret, and will love Him, possess Him in secret, and delight in Him in secret. (St John of the Cross, *Spiritual Canticle*, 1:10-11)

You must also close the gate to your imagination. This is much more difficult! Every time you pray in silence, the "home cinema" is turned on. You want to think about Jesus and suddenly you find you are at work, at your studies, in the supermarket, on your holidays! You go back to contemplating but within a minute you are planning your afternoon tasks. And so on…

Imagination is like a vicious horse which flings up its heels; it insists on showing scenes from the outside life although your eyes are closed. What do you do then? You do not want that! Despite all of this, keep praying! Even if it seems you are distracted for most of the time. It is only your imagination which is taking a walk. Your *will* and your *heart* are with God.

Perhaps you can do something more. You can become a friend to your distractions. Look at them in a positive way. Use them!

> The biggest misunderstanding is the thought that your distractions are a sign that you are unable to pray. What does it mean if you have a hundred and one distractions during your half hour of prayer? It means that each time you turn your back on your distractions, you are turning to God. It means that a hundred and one times, you say "NO" to yourself and "YES" to God; a hundred and one times, you act with unselfish love, helping "the old self" to die in order for the "new self" to be born in you.
> (D. Torkington, *Prophet: The Inner Meaning of Prayer*)

Distractions teach you to be humble! They teach you that, while you pray, almost everything depends on God and you can offer only faithfulness and openness to His actions. They remind you that you are the hurt one who constantly seeks healing from God, the Doctor.

Distractions also show you the areas of your selfishness; the areas which need to be cleansed. If you are thinking about a problem, for instance, the exam you failed, it means that you are thinking about yourself and you haven't placed everything in God's hands. If you imagine yourself wandering the streets of your city, it means that it gives you more pleasure than following Jesus. If you are tempted and have "impure thoughts" it might be that you do not want to place this secret frailty in God's hands.

Distractions are useful if they help to inflame your great desires. They help you to see how far you are from being united with Jesus. Do not be discouraged but call to Him, from the bottom of your heart, to come and take you in His arms.

You see? From being a big obstacle, distractions can become your great friends in silent prayer!

Finally, I have good news for you. St Teresa of Avila said that we will always have distractions in our life on earth. This saint, who was an inspirational guide to the spiritual life, admitted that throughout eighteen years, she was forced many times to keep hold of the bench while she was praying in order not to run away from the chapel. If it didn't stop her from achieving "spiritual matrimony" with the Beloved, it means that you can receive that gift as well! Everything depends on one thing: PERSEVERANCE!

Therefore I ask you: Stay! Remain in this crucial "nothing" with your eyes closed but your heart open to the action of that Power which transforms and burns you.

6. Looking at Jesus

While you are trying to look at Jesus, He, and not your pre-occupations, is the centre of your prayer.

It is He who is praying inside you to the Father.

It is He who is constantly begotten inside you through His Father.

It is He who is constantly acting as a gift to His Father.

In the depths of your soul, the Son and the Father are ONE and united in the love of the Holy Spirit.

Look at Him through the eyes of your faith.

This is exactly what contemplation is: "It is looking at Jesus through faith" (St John of the Cross).

The fourth "nothing" is turning your sight from yourself and turning it to Jesus.

Here, it is as though you are in Heaven. Once there, you will look at Jesus face to face, without any curtain and you will wonder at the great love of the Son for His Father. You will look and look forever and ever.

But you can experience this already here on earth. You can experience this every day! Although you cannot yet see Him clearly, as though only in a mirror, nevertheless, you do see Him *in reality*! St Teresa of Avila encouraged her sisters to do that: "I am not asking you now to think of Him, or to form numerous conceptions of Him, or to make subtle meditations with your understanding. I am asking you only to look at Him." (St Teresa of Avila, *The Way of Perfection*, 26)

You can look at God in two ways.

You can use your imagination. After reading the fragment of the Gospel, try to imagine it in your soul. Pretend that all you read about is happening inside you. Look at Jesus, for example when He is chatting to the Samaritan woman. Imagine Him sitting thirsty by the well in the hot afternoon and waiting for someone. Suddenly the woman comes along, weak and sinful, as we will soon find out. Jesus turns to her and speaks: "Give me a drink…" Read their conversation carefully and try to picture the scene.

Then take the next step: try to imagine that *you are* this Samaritan woman… Your soul is "married" to five "men", representing your senses which dominate your whole life. You have never thought about entering your inner life where your Beloved dwells. Despite the fact that you have been unfaithful and you have given yourself to others, He does not stop talking to you because He is desperate for your love. He is still waiting for you by the well and showing you the real depths where He wants to draw you. What is more, He is revealing the secret of His life, telling you that true worshippers should worship God *in spirit and in truth*. He simply wants you! You can look at Him like this in every scene written in the Gospel.

However for many, this type of contemplation is difficult and sometimes impossible. Instead of helping, the imagination proves to be disruptive and makes it impossible to contemplate any text. The more one tries the more difficult it becomes. So a second way of looking at Jesus becomes helpful, without imagination or comparison. It is *simply looking at Jesus.*

Simply looking at Jesus does not require any pictures or scenes. On the contrary - it is a simple straightforward look, without any curtain and without any assistance. It is looking at God leading His internal life in your soul. This is like seeking the invisible by "*looking with your heart*". There is nothing familiar in our everyday life to explain this second way of looking at Jesus. It can only be understood by someone who has experienced it. If you are convinced that you cannot meditate, then it is the right time to start looking at Jesus in this particular way. Do not even try to use the imagination but run straight to the finishing line, to God. Do not imagine Him but BE WITH HIM, IN HIM!

Never seek to satisfy yourself with what you comprehend of God, but rather with what you comprehend not; and never rest on the love of, and delight in, that which you can understand and feel, but rather on that which is beyond your understanding and feeling. God is inaccessible and hidden, and though it may seem that you have found Him, felt Him, and comprehended Him, yet you must ever regard Him as hidden, serve Him as hidden, in secret. Do not be like many unwise, who, with low views of God, think that when they cannot comprehend Him, or be conscious of His presence, that He is then farther away and more hidden, when the contrary is true, namely, that He is nearer to them when they are least aware of it. Thus, when you are near to Him, the very infirmity of your vision makes the darkness palpable. (St John of the Cross, *Spiritual Canticle*, 1:16-17)

So, if you find it difficult to "look at Jesus", be happy because that means you now possess Him! If you are looking at the Sun, do not be surprised if you can't see anything!

You are very close to being united with Jesus; just a stone's throw away.

Everything we have learned so far has been an introduction to what is the most important element in silent prayer: the fifth and final "nothing", which is THE ACT OF FAITH.

This is where the soul and the Beloved meet.

The act of faith is the act of entire unity.

You are at the summit!

In the act of faith the happiness of Jesus reaches its summit and He Himself is in ecstasy.

It is all thanks to you!

Because the act of faith is something very special, let me tell you about it more particularly in the next chapters.

PART TWO:
THE ACT OF FAITH

Faith is the single most suitable means of uniting the soul and God. (St John of the Cross)

7. The act of faith in silent prayer

Silent prayer leads to the ACT OF FAITH. In the act of faith man unites with God.

Everything we have learned so far has led us to the fifth and final "nothing". Here the Beloved gives himself entirely to the bride and the bride to Him. Here the words of the Song of Songs are fulfilled: "My beloved is mine and I am his" (*Sg* 2:16).

This is the complete union which transforms the soul into God's image.

What is the act of faith in silent prayer?

It is being ready to forget about yourself and open your heart for God to enter and rule. It is the commitment of the bride who keeps nothing for herself, but gives up everything for the *Beloved*.

This act can be accomplished by:

Silence and by being convinced that you are in God and God is in you just like a man and his wife who are united in the act of love. They are for each other and in each other entirely. They remain one body and soul.

"For the spiritual person...silence and God seem to be identified." (P. Marie-Eugen OCD, *I Want to See God*, III,5,A)

Concentration and accepting God through your whole being just as a sponge absorbs water. It is like listening to your favourite Mozart concerto or looking at a Monet painting in an empty gallery. You are focusing totally on what you are listening to or looking at; nothing else matters! It is just you and God. You are united!

Short phrases, which can act as the "*cry of the soul*", expressing faith, love and utter devotion:

"I believe in You!"

"I am all Yours!"

"I love You!"

"I give myself entirely to You!"

"I trust You!"

"Draw me and we will run together!" Etc.

Each soul will find its own words to address to God, the Trinity. Do not be afraid to say them! These are the only words to say while praying! They express yourself and your willingness to be open to God and to hold back nothing of yourself. He needs these words! He is happy to hear them because He has found the soul willing to give itself entirely to Him.

The act of faith is something mystical and very difficult to explain, especially for those who are not familiar with the spiritual life. Words are not adequate here. Descriptions and analogies from the human world are mere reflections of what is happening between the soul and the Beloved in a different and supernatural dimension. Perhaps that is why all the great mystics used poetic language to describe this relationship. This is how it was described in one of the most beautiful books of the Old Testament: the *Song of Songs*.

Beloved: - "How beautiful you are, my Beloved, how beautiful you are! Our bed is the greensward".

Bride: - "I found him whom my soul loves. I held him, and would not let him go!"

Beloved: - "You ravish my heart, my sister, my promised bride; you ravish my heart with a single one of your glances. How delicious is your love, more delicious than wine!"

Bride: - "Let my love come into his garden, let him taste its most exquisite fruits! I belong to my love, and his desire is for me".

If you want to understand the act of love in silent prayer do it *every day*! You will soon find out that you cannot live without it! According to St John of the Cross, the act of faith is the only way to unite the soul with God. This is how St Thérèse of Lisieux expresses it:

With me prayer is an uplifting of the heart; a glance towards Heaven; a cry of gratitude and love, uttered equally in sorrow and in joy. In a word, it is something noble, supernatural, which expands my soul and unites it to God. (St Thérèse of Lisieux, *Manuscript C*, 25r°-v°)

It is important to mention that these words occur in part IV of the *Catechism of the Catholic Church* which deals with prayer. It is as though these words provide a summary of the whole study of Christian prayer.

Nobody, neither you nor I, is excluded from the possibility of sharing this joy provided we accept that, if we create no boundaries, God will act in us.

8. The act of faith - the example of the woman who had a flow of blood

Silent prayer has its source in Jesus Christ. If you read the Bible carefully, you will find it described in many places. There is a very beautiful account in St Mark's Gospel:

Now there was a woman who had suffered from the haemorrhage for twelve years; after long and painful treatment under various doctors, she had spent all she had without being any better for it; in fact she was getting worse. She had heard about Jesus, and she came up through the crowd and touched his cloak from behind, thinking, "If I can just touch his clothes, I shall be saved". And at once the source of the bleeding dried up, and she felt in herself that she was cured of her complaint. And at once aware of the power that had gone out from him, Jesus turned round in the crowd and said, "Who touched my clothes?" His disciples said to him, "You see how the crowd is pressing round you; how can you ask, 'Who touched me?'" But he continued to look round to see who had done it. Then the woman came forward, frightened and trembling because she knew what had happened to her, and she fell at his feet and told him the whole truth. "My daughter," he said, "your faith has restored you to health; go in peace, and be free of your complaint." (*Mk* 5:25-34)

You are probably wondering where silent prayer is mentioned in that description.

Read it with your spirit; use your "eyes of faith" and you will notice silent prayer in every sentence of that description.

Who is the anonymous woman who had a flow of blood? It is you and me and all the other souls who are dying if separated from Jesus.

There is no need to look for healing from various "doctors" in workshops, travel, material goods, family, lovers, work, physical pleasure, healthy living or anything else that distracts us from our pain. After many years this woman had become no better but had grown worse. And then...

And then we see how silent prayer, the real journey towards unity with Jesus, can begin. The starting point is the first "nothing" - reflection and concentration which enables the soul to take the correct path with no outside distractions. Then the soul enters *within* just as the sick woman did.

"She had heard about Jesus" - but from whom? We are not told. Perhaps she had heard about Jesus from a friend or from one of her relatives who had seen Him and His miracles. Perhaps this friend or relative had spoken to Jesus, maybe had even experienced healing. All this might have been reported to her and she *listened* with great attention. How can we find meaning here? This is the second "nothing" where the soul reads or hears about Jesus. Here, the soul finds out about Him, learns about Him from someone's witness.

And what happened next? Being alone in her own house she "closed her eyes", the gates to her senses, and she started to think. She imagined Jesus, His disciples, and the many sick people who were healed by Jesus. She imagined the background to the events which took place on the banks of the Galilean Lake. She had a kind of a brain storm from which one idea emerged. At first this idea did not trouble her but soon it became very persistent and almost irrational:

"Perhaps *I* should…? Maybe Jesus is waiting *for me…?* Maybe He is waiting over there *for me…?*"

What happened next became a turning point in this woman's life. Perhaps she debated her "for" and "against" arguments. Perhaps she hesitated… She might have told herself that such things did not happen in the real world. However, the third "nothing" left her with no excuses. She submitted in the end. She made the decision and she went to meet Jesus.

"The soul that will go out of the house of its own will, and abandon the bed of its own satisfaction, will find the divine Wisdom, the Son of God, the Bridegroom waiting at the door without." (St John of the Cross, *Spiritual Canticle*, 3:4)

When she got near, the first thing she saw was the crowd pressing around Him, surrounding Him so she could not see Him.

"Look? Why did you come here? You should have stayed at home! It is not real!"

This happens in silent prayer as well, when you see your target on the horizon it disappears from your sight. Your target is surrounded by the "crowd" of outside feelings which makes you vulnerable and makes you give up your initial decision. These distractions say: "This is not for you!" They want you to stop and go back to where you were. However, the woman-soul-lover is determined. She does not give up.

"There must be some kind of solution! If I can just touch his clothes".

Slowly, with a huge effort, she presses her way towards Him. She does not give up although she is constantly jostled by the crowd. She has her eyes set on Jesus; this gives her the strength to hold on to the right path. She keeps looking at Him and in that way she attains the fourth "nothing". She is very close, only a few steps more! She can feel Him close. And then… *She touches His cloak.*

The result is immediate! Jesus *feels* and the woman *feels*! He perceives in Himself that power had gone forth from Him; she feels in her body that she has been healed of her disease.

"Who touched my clothes?" - He asks looking for the one, the mad one!

Although everybody is pressing around Him, He knows that somebody has touched Him differently - touched Him with FAITH. Soon He will confirm it by saying: "My daughter, your faith has restored you to health". He will point out what it was that made Him give Himself to her.

This is silent prayer. *This is touching God by the act of faith which connects man's soul with God.* When you pray you go through each step that this woman went through. Then you approach the fifth "nothing" where you give yourself to God and He gives Himself to you.

This is why the act of faith cannot be confined to a short period of time. It must last for half an hour or possibly longer. Otherwise you will not be there with Jesus; you will have stopped half way along your journey and gone back home, not even knowing what you have lost.

And now let's go together to Jesus!

9. The act of faith - confidence

The first and the most important feature of faith, is *confidence*. Whenever you act in faith you *always* reach God! The relationship between the soul and the Beloved is always successful! It cannot be otherwise! When you touch fire, your fingers will be burned. When you touch a balloon with a needle, it will burst, releasing the air trapped inside. When you dive into God with your faith, God will be with you pouring His life into your soul. What's more - He is *compelled* to do that!!! He is overwhelmed. He is like crystal water from where you may take as much as you can, following the example of the bride from the *Song of Songs*: "I found him whom my soul loves. I held him, and would not let him go!" (*Sg* 3:4)

This happens because faith is the first of the theological virtues which are of *the same nature as God*. In faith you are "at the same level" as God. You cannot say the same about any other attempt that man makes to reach God, no matter how worthy. Disciplining the body, exercising reason in the knowledge of God and making fervent acts of will are only steps taken by man. You can think about God for hours, you can envisage prospects for your future, make resolutions concerning moral behaviour and do spiritual exercises but unless you make the act of *faith* you will not reach the summit. You will be like the crowd gathered around Jesus; none of them affected Him because they lacked faith. Although they were pressing against Him, He couldn't feel anything. Jesus said about them: "I have never known you" (*Mt* 7:23).

Consider what happens with a good guitar string. If there is another one alongside which is of a similar note, they will vibrate together, recognising the same frequency and leaving all the rest in silence. God acts in a very similar way. He recognises the soul which imitates His never-ending frequency of self-giving. This is what He feels and He immediately does the same; He gives Himself for that soul. That is why only the theological virtues can link you to the Holy Trinity who lives in your soul.

God is love. Complete union will happen *in love*, in His house, on the other side of life. You will see Him then "naked", unveiled, face to face, in His "dressing room" as Eckhart wrote. Here, in this life, He is covered by His "garment". That is why *faith* is so important here on earth. Faith gives you the same result as love. Faith allows you to receive God entirely. *Hope* is the servant of love and faith and together they cross the borders of this world and link them together beyond. "These remain: faith, hope and love, the three of them; and the greatest of them is love". (*1 Co* 13:13)

Having the confidence of faith does not mean that you will obtain everything you want from God. He does not give you health, relief from pain or an easy life. God does not guarantee that you will pass your exam, find a job or your life partner. If you come to Him having that selfish attitude, He will not recognise you. You will not achieve anything by being selfish and having your own plans for life.

He promises nothing but *only Himself!* Nothing more! But what a gift He gives!

Every day He will give you His interior life! And you begin to look like Him, to think like Him, to act like Him.

You will be brave and sensible like Him. You will want to serve and give yourself as He does, even to the last drop of your blood. You will only want to do His will. Everything else will be irrelevant to you. You will be returning to your primary self, the one who was originally created by God.

This is the effect of the act of faith.

> In supernatural contemplation the soul, like a mirror exposed to the rays of the sun, is all aglow with the light of the divine Sun that shines upon souls; like a sponge immersed in the ocean, it is permeated with pure waters from the Fountain of living water; like the log thrown into a fire, it too is transformed into fire by the all-consuming Fire which is God. (P. Marie-Eugen OCD, *I Want to See God*, III,7,B,II)

10. The act of faith - darkness

Faith has a second feature. According to St John of the Cross, faith is *dark*.

> Faith can be compared to midnight. The excess of light which comes from faith is dark for the soul. The soul has to be emptied, has to be detached and has to be in the dark. The soul needs to walk like a blind man beside faith which acts as a guiding light. The blind man relies on nothing which he can taste or imagine. (St John of the Cross, *Ascent of Mount Carmel*, 2:2-4)

What is described here is difficult. We yearn to be with God in the light. We long to "see", feel, and experience God's presence. This is why we tend to look for signs of His presence and listen for voices which might show us the right path. We search for spiritual feelings which we believe are evidence of God's presence. We are eager to hear about revelations - shadows of Jesus, His Mother or other saints reflected on some tree or wall. When these signs are lacking, we turn to a variety of things, sensual or emotional, which we think will make us happy. We would like God to uplift us spiritually while we are praying. We would like God to give us joy and peace and to fulfil our wishes. What we must realise is that this is seeking oneself through prayer and not God.

If you want to be united with your Beloved, you must leave everything behind! Not only should you not think about what you are feeling but you should avoid your feelings as if they were a trap. Enter the darkness because there you will find Him, the one you are looking for. As John of the Cross teaches: "Spiritual night is faith without any light. It is the real path leading to God. In order to entirely unite with Him through love and blessing, you have to go into the darkness and leave everything you can see, hear or imagine." (St John of the Cross, *Ascent of Mount Carmel*, 2:1-4)

This means you have to concede that you may experience nothing while you are praying. This is what makes you different from the woman with the haemorrhage. She experienced recovery from her illness - you will not experience that! The connection between your soul and God through the act of faith happens *on the spiritual level.* This is a level which human senses or feelings cannot reach. This proves to be the most difficult thing to grasp. This is perhaps why only very few people decide to pray every day in silence. Man prefers light and spiritual happiness, even at the price of departing from God.

Notice that everything marvellous and beautiful in the Bible takes place at night.

Israel left Egypt at night.

Jesus was born at night.

Jesus ate His last supper with His disciples at night.

Jesus arose from death at night.

You will also find Him at night.

> Upon my bed by night I sought him whom my soul loves; I sought him, but found him not. I will rise now and go about the city, in the streets and in the squares; I will seek him whom my soul loves. The watchmen found me, as they went about in the city. "Have you seen him whom my soul loves?" Scarcely had I passed them, when I found him whom my soul loves. *(Sg 3:1-4)*

So then, look for God! Do not look for yourself. By leaving all affections and passions behind you when you pray, you show that you are prepared to forget entirely about yourself. You show that you do not treat God as a "milking cow" as Eckhart said; you show that all you long for is to make God happy.

11. God is touched by the act of faith

The fact that you do not feel anything when you make your act of faith does not mean that God does not feel anything. On the contrary, He does! He immediately feels your touch which targets Him like an arrow of love. He responds immediately: "Who touched my clothes?" - He asks. "Attacked" by your courage, God is shocked that somebody is brave enough to get so far. He is stunned! He is bewitched by your act of trust in Him. This is reflected in the *Song of Songs*:

How beautiful you are, my beloved,
how beautiful you are!
You ravish my heart,
my sister, my promised bride;
you ravish my heart
with a single one of your glances,
with a single link of your necklace.
What spells lie in your love,
my sister, my promised bride.
How delicious is your love, more delicious than wine!
(*Sg* 4:1,9-10)

It is amazing that you can surprise God in this way! The only one to succeed is the one who trusts in God entirely!

The following example illustrates this: "When Jesus heard these words, he was astonished at him and, turning round, said to the crowd following him, 'I tell you, not even in Israel have I found faith as great as this'." (*Lk* 7:9)

In this example Jesus shows what it is that allows you to delight Him - it is FAITH.

Above all your trust must be entire which means putting yourself into His hands unconditionally, without any "but". The soul, brave enough to do this, targets God's heart as if firing a dart into it! This makes God most happy! He is defenceless! He is in a state of ecstasy! He is completely in love! He is in love at first sight! "You are wholly beautiful, my Beloved, and without a blemish." (*Sg* 4:7)

The act of faith is like a kiss on the lips of the Beloved. "Ah, why are you not my brother, nursed at my mother's breast! Then if I met you out of doors, I could kiss you without people thinking ill of me." (*Sg* 8:1)

This is how God reacts after being touched by the act of love. God FEELS this act of love directed to Him, transmitted to Him at His own level - the spiritual level. He is the Spirit.

And what else is happening to Him in this very moment? His Son is begotten. The birth of the Son is a perpetual act which is intensely renewed in the soul that has given itself to the Trinity.

This act takes place in the eternal present. It happens in that very instant. The Son of God is being born constantly. God is a "giving birth" because He is the Trinity. Each soul, according to its own ability and faith, attracts the Word and receives it in itself. He - the Word - wants to actualise the mystery of His incarnation in everyone. (A. Gozier, *The Birth of God in the Soul*)

When you make the act of faith, you are repeating the words of Mary, "Let it be done unto me according to thy Word" and the Son of God is immediately born in your soul. There He finds His new placenta where He is conceived and He can live! "God finds His joy in generating; that is why He generates His Son in our soul, so we have a full joy in it as well." (Eckhart, *Sermon 59*)

By His death, the Son gives Himself to His Father. This is another result of the act of faith. He does not keep anything for Himself but He gives everything. GIVING is His nature, He gives everything to the very end. He gives Himself until He loses Himself.

At the very same moment He is raised from the dead by His Father. God is Life and He does not allow the sanctity of His Son to be contaminated by death.

The Son is born, He dies and is raised at the same time!

This is not the last of the miracles which happen in the soul! "Christ is ascending into Heaven in the faithful man. He is ascending from the very bottom of man's heart into the outside, the domain of the human being, up to the borders of human conscience." (A. Gozier, *The Birth of God in the Soul*)

Your soul becomes Heaven for God. He finds His home there. He feels himself there. Finally He is at home! Finally He is in His Heaven. You are His Heaven!

Here the Trinity is living to the full! The Father is contemplating His Son, and the Son is responding with equal love to Him. They are both breathing the Holy Spirit.

This breathing of the Holy Spirit in the soul, whereby God transforms it in Himself, is to the soul a joy so deep, so exquisite, and so grand that no mortal tongue can describe it, no human understanding, as such, conceive it in any degree; for even that which passes in the soul with respect to the communication which takes place in its transformation wrought in this life cannot be described, because the soul united with God and transformed in Him breathes in God that very divine aspiration which God breathes Himself in the soul when it is transformed in Him. (St John of the Cross, *Spiritual Canticle*, 39:2)

In the act of union you become one with God, the Holy Trinity. As St Paul says, "Anyone who attaches himself to the Lord is one spirit with Him" (*1 Co* 6:17).

In this union God gives Himself to the soul and, with great glory, He transforms the soul so that both God and the soul are one. They are one just like flames reflected in glass, like coal and fire, like the light coming from the stars and the sun. God spreads to the soul just like fluid spreads to all the veins. To be even more precise it is the soul's transformation in God. (St John of the Cross, *Spiritual Canticle*, 26:3-4)

This is what happens every day when you perform the act of faith. Is this not enough for you? "O souls created for this and called to this, what are you doing? What are your occupations?" (St John of the Cross, *Spiritual Canticle*, 29:8)

12. Trust: The act of faith in everyday life

If you spend at least half an hour every day on your journey to God and connect with Him through your faith, your prayer lasts for the rest of the day. It will slowly change your way of life - your conversations, thoughts, and deeds. Every day your faith, which allows you to touch Jesus, will become a constant interior disposition which will lead to total *trust*. You will see everything from a different angle and in different colours. It is like looking through the eyes of Jesus and not your own. It is like seeing with the values of Jesus in mind.

You will recognise something exceptional in *everyone* you meet on your way. Everyone is sent by God for you! If people are unfriendly and difficult to deal with, then you will be willing to greet them with your smile, acceptance, a good word and a friendly gesture. If they are friends, you will be able to talk to them about important things and not just make small talk. You will help them to grow. You will be gentle but also you will raise your voice if necessary just as Jesus sometimes did.

Every *event* which once disturbed you will now be seen as God's inspiration. God will speak to you through events. Illness, suffering, loss of somebody close to you - this is all God's touch and He is asking you not to mourn but to forget about yourself and give everything to Him, even to the last drop. Admiration, privilege - these are opportunities to be humble and silent; an invitation for you to serve someone else even more than before. Success, failure, acceptance or rejection - you should take all of them in the name of faith, knowing that God's will is hidden behind these events. Then, even a sin will makes sense - "positive" sense! Work, rest, study, happiness and sadness - all these will have their place and will be shared with God who is living in your soul. You will be able to see His presence everywhere. You will feel that He is urging you not to lose a single moment but to use everything He gives you creatively. Despite all of this, it is amazing that your life will remain so normal! There will be no visible changes. "A person who lives in complete surrender to God's will does the same thing night and day. He prays, eats breakfast, works, speaks or relaxes, but he knows, above all, that he is doing God's will." (J. Chapman, *Spiritual Letters*)

This is what constant prayer is; it is living in the presence of God. This is the result of your daily presence with Him in the act of trust which leads to a sensitive and alert disposition.

There are three steps to follow to achieve complete unity with God.

First, you gain the ability to *accept His will.* Where you first fought against Him, telling Him about your plans and asking Him to realise them, now you put your weapons down, knowing that nothing depends on you but everything depends on Him. You are beginning to live according to the logic taught by St Paul:

> Can anything cut us off from the love of Christ? - Can hardships or distress, or persecution, or lack of food and clothing, or threats or violence?... No; we come through all these things triumphantly victorious, by the power of him who loved us. For I am certain of this: neither death nor life, nor angels, nor principalities, nothing already in existence and nothing still to come, nor any power, nor the heights, nor the depths, nor any created thing whatever, will be able to come between us and the love of God, known to us in Christ Jesus our Lord. (*Rm* 8:35-39)

In the second step you start, not only passively to accept everything that God gives you, but you begin actively to *co-operate* with Him. You are obedient to His will. "The second stage consists of the aspect of God's will that gives us something to do and that comes with concrete tasks to be done. To say 'yes, Father' here means putting one's hand to the plough, being God's obedient servant." (W. Stinissen, *Into Your Hands, Father*)

By following the second step you can see that every moment brings its own task or, to be precise, every moment brings the invitation from God for you to do something positive. St Thérèse of Lisieux was the champion in being alert to God's voice. In *Manuscript B* she recorded her motto:

> Yes, my Beloved, this is how my life is going to be consumed… To prove my love to you, I have no other way but to throw flowers. This means I will not waste any tiny surrender, nor any other look or word. I will make use of all little things and do them with love. (St Thérèse of Lisieux, *Manuscript B*, 4r°-4v°)

In her case these words were followed up by deeds. She transformed them into life. At the end of her short but very intense life she could say: "Now trust is my only guide. I do not have another compass. I cannot pray intensely for anything else but that God's will may happen in me" (*Manuscript A*, 83r°).

In the third step of trust your "I" disappears and God takes its place. God is shining through you. *Man becomes His instrument* and repeats after St Paul: "It is no longer I, but Christ living in me" (*Ga* 2:20).

Man does not insist on anything but lives "with the speed of the Holy Trinity" (M.D. Molinié).
People who look at him see Jesus.

Jesus is no longer hidden in the shadow of the man.
The Holy Spirit acts through him spreading His gifts.
But man remains himself! He is himself entirely!
Everything he does is blessed by God and man is not selfish any more.
Man wants the same as God wants.
Man thinks like Him.
Reacts like Him.
Speaks like Him.
Acts like Him.
This is how everyday prayer in silence changes your life.

And now you can only pray using the words of Charles de Foucauld:

Father,
I abandon myself into Your hands;
Do with me what You will.
For whatever You may do I thank You.

I am ready for all,
I accept all.

Let only your will to be done in me,
as in all Your creatures.
I wish no more than this, O Lord.

Into Your hands I commend my soul.
I offer it to you
with all the love of my heart.

For I love you, my God,
And so need to give myself
To surrender myself
into Your hands,
without reserve,
and with boundless confidence,
for you are my Father.

SILENT PRAYER

We are not accustomed to spending time with God, in silence, without any specific words or intentions. We feel more comfortable saying something! We feel we must tell him about the Church's needs, the world's needs, our own needs. Then we feel we have achieved something; we have not wasted our time. Silent prayer obliges us to leave all that to the Almighty. To enter into silent prayer we must leave everything behind. Learning how to pray is possible and a way of living that supports a deep and happy Christian faith.

Fr Andrzej Muszala is a priest of Krakow diocese, and professor of bioethics and medical ethics.

D810   £2.50

ISBN 978-1-78469-130-1